GET  MAKOTO+

EVERY MONTH AUTOMATICALLY
(and at a discount)

https://www.MakotoPlus.com

You'll get:

Download the Latest Makoto Issue | Weekly Lessons | Reusable TheJapanShop.com Coupon | Monthly Freebies

MAKOTO

THEJAPANSHOP.COM
VOLUME 5 | ISSUE 54 | August 2022

e-zine for learners of Japanese

こうにゅう
ご 購入
ありがとう
ございます。

Thank you so much
for your purchase!

WHO ARE WE?

Over two decades ago, Clay & Yumi began **TheJapanesePage.com**, one of the Internet's oldest and largest *free* Japanese instructional sites with hundreds of free articles for beginners of Japanese.

They also maintain **TheJapanShop.com**, a web-store specializing in materials to help learners of Japanese.

Have any questions or comments? Contact us at **help@thejapanshop.com**

We just released our newest Makoto+ course. It is on Japanese Idioms. At the moment, it covers about 80 idioms in three modules, but as we did with the Japanese Names Course, we will continue to release modules every few weeks until the course covers over 300 super useful idioms. Check out our Makoto+ online courses here:

https://makotoplus.com/makoto-courses/

If you are a Shogun or Lifetime Makoto+ member, the Makoto+ courses are all free—included in your membership. If you are a Samurai member, you can find a coupon in your members area to buy any course for only $10, or you can upgrade to Shogun or Lifetime.

We have plans for many more courses on subjects that are useful for the student of Japanese but not often covered by textbooks.

For example, katakana English—words originally from (or based off) English. Sometimes the meaning is what a native English speaker would expect, but usually… it's not. However, the tricky part isn't the meaning even when it is very different from its English counterpart. The most headache-inducing aspect is the pronunciation. Does マクドナルド sound anything remotely like "McDonald's"?!

We are planning courses on topics such as this. Useful, but not often covered in textbooks or other learning resources.

Thank you!
Clay & Yumi

P.S. The cover says, めぐみです。よろしく！ *megumi desu. yoroshiku!* which means, "I'm Megumi. Pleased to meet ya!" This character was drawn by our daughter, Megumi!

In this Issue:

- **Laughs, Jokes, Riddles, and Puns**
- **Vocabulary: 顔から火が出る**
- **Prefecture Spotlight: Kanagawa**
- **Etymology: 王国と帝国の違い**
- **Anime Phrase of the Day**
- **Haiku：松尾芭蕉**
- **Kanji Spotlight: 月**
- **Grammar Time! の as a pronoun**
- **Japanese Readers: Cold meals (beginner) + The History of Anime (Intermediate)**

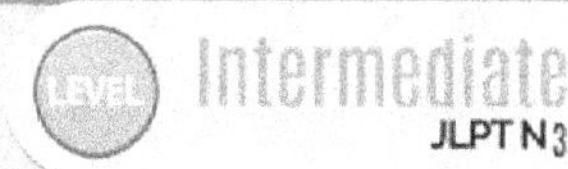

LEVEL **Intermediate**
JLPT N3

Scan for Recording

駅の自動販売機でジュースを買おうとしたら、なぜかオロナミンC（栄養ドリンク）が出てきた。もう一度お金を入れてジュースを買おうとボタンを押しても、またオロナミンCが出てきたので、これはおかしいと文句を言おうと駅員さんのそばに行って「あのこれ・・・」と声をかけた。すると、駅員さんは満面の笑顔になったので、つい「いつもお疲れ様です。」と言ってオロナミンCを手渡してしまった。

When I tried to buy juice (or soda) from a vending machine at a train station, for some reason Oronamin C (an energy drink) came out. I put money in the machine again and although I pressed the button to buy juice, Oronamin C came out again. So, I went to the station attendant to complain that something is wrong with the machine, and began with, "Um, this…" Then, seeing the station attendant's huge smile, without thought I handed him a bottle of Oronamin C and said, "Thank you always for your hard work."

Vocabulary:

ジョーク *jo-ku*—a joke

駅の自動販売機で *eki no jidouhanbaiki de*—at a train station's vending machine [駅 (railway

Vocabulary Continued

station; train station; station) + **の** ('s; of; modifier) + **自動販売機** (vending machine) + **で** (at; indicates the location of action)]

ジュースを買おうとしたら *juusu o kaou to shitara*—when (I) tried to buy juice [**ジュース** (juice) + **を** (indicates the direct object of action) + **買おう** (plain volitional form of **買う** (to buy; to purchase); volitional form is used when the speaker initiates an act or intends to do something) + **としたら** (from **とする** (to try to ...; to be about to do ...; to decide to ...); ~**ら** means "when; if; after"; how to form: Verb (**た** form) + **ら**)]

なぜか *naze ka*—somehow; for some reason; without knowing why

オロナミンC（栄養ドリンク）が出てきた *oronamin C (eiyou dorinku) ga dete kita*—Oronamin C (energy drink) came out [**オロナミンC** (Oronamin C) + **栄養ドリンク** (energy drink; nutritional supplement drink; vitamin drink; **栄養** (nutrition; nourishment) + **ドリンク** (drink)) + **が** (identifies what performs the action) + **出てきた** (came out; plain past form of **出てくる** (to come out; to appear))]

もう一度 *mou ichido*—once more; again

お金を入れて *okane o irete*—put the money, and [**お金** (money) + **を** (indicates the direct object of action) + **入れて** (put and; **て**-form of **入れる** (to put in) which is used to connect to the next phrase, creating the meaning of "and")]

ジュースを買おう *juusu o kaou*—intend to buy a juice; (I'll) buy a juice [**ジュース** (juice; this can also mean soda) + **を** (indicates the direct object of action) + **買おう** (plain volitional form of **買う** (to buy; to purchase))]

と *to*—upon doing so [shows that the part of the sentence right before **と** is a condition or cause, and the other part of the sentence is a result]

Vocabulary Continued

ボタンを押しても *botan o oshite mo*—although (I) pressed the button [**ボタン** (button; push-button) + **を** (indicates the direct object of action) + **押しても** (although (I) pressed; ~**も** means "even; although; even if; even though"; how to form: Verb **て**-form + **も**)]

またオロナミンCが出てきた *mata oronamin C ga dete kita*—Oronamin C came out again [**また** (again; once more; once again) + **オロナミンC** (Oronamin C) + **が** (identifies what performs the action; emphasizes the preceding word) + **出てきた** (came out; plain past form of **出てくる** (to come out; to appear))]

ので *node*—because of ...; the reason is ...; so; since

これはおかしいと文句を言おうと *kore wa okashii to monku o iou to*—intend to complain that something is wrong with this (machine) [**これ** (this) + **は** (indicates the sentence topic) + **おかしい** (strange; something is wrong) + **と** (used for quoting (thoughts, speech, etc.)) + **文句** (complaint; grumbling; objection) + **を** (indicates the direct object of action) + **言おう** (plain volitional form of **言う** (to say; to utter; to declare)) + **と** (shows that the part of the sentence right before **と** is a condition or cause, and the other part of the sentence is a result)]

駅員さんのそばに行って *ekiin san no soba ni itte*—went to the station attendant, and [**駅員さん** ((train) station attendant; station employee; station staff; **さん** is a politeness marker and is used after a noun) + **の** (is used to tell the location) + **そば** (near; close; beside; vicinity) + **に** (expresses the direction and destination) + **行って** (went and; **て**-form of **行く** (to go) which is used to connect to the next phrase, creating the meaning of "and")]

「あのこれ・・・」 *「ano kore...」*—"Um, this..." [**「」** (quotation marks; " ") + **あの** (um; uh (hesitation); excuse me; you know) + **これ** (this)]

「あのこれ・・・」と声をかけた *「ano kore...」 to koe o kaketa*—started talking, "Um, this..." [**「あの**

Vocabulary Continued

これ・・・」 ("Um, this...") + と (quotation marker; used for quoting speech) + 声をかけた (started talking; plain past form of 声をかける (to start talking (to); to call out (to)))]

すると *suru to*—then; and

満面の笑顔になった *manmen no egao ni natta*—became a full smile; smiled a big beaming smile [満面 (the whole face; (wearing an expression) all over one's face) + の (modifier) + 笑顔 (smiling face; smile) + になった (became; plain past form of になる (become; come to; turn out))]

つい *tsui*—without thought; against one's better judgment [is used when you do things unintentionally, carelessly, or by accident]

いつもお疲れ様です *itsumo otsukaresama desu*—thank you always for your hard work [いつも (always; all the time; at all times) + お疲れ様 (thank you (for your hard work); good work) + です (be; is)]

「いつもお疲れ様です。」と言って 「*itsumo otsukaresama desu.*」 *to itte*—said, "Thank you always for your hard work." [「いつもお疲れ様です。」 ("Thank you always for your hard work.") + と (quotation marker) + 言って (said; て-form of 言う (to say; to utter) which is used to connect to the next phrase)]

オロナミンCを手渡してしまった *oronamin C o tewatashite shimatta*—handed (him) a bottle of Oronamin C [オロナミンC (Oronamin C) + を (indicates the direct object of action) + 手渡して しまった (from 手渡す (to hand over); ~てしまった is the plain past form of ~てしまう (is used when you do things unintentionally) and is often used with つい (unintentionally; subconsciously; by mistake))]

VOCABULARY

Learn Useful Words, Phrases, and Sayings

Scan for Recording

<ruby>顔<rt>かお</rt></ruby>から<ruby>火<rt>ひ</rt></ruby>が<ruby>出<rt>で</rt></ruby>る

kao kara hi ga deru

burn with shame; be embarrassed

ⓘ Use this idiom when your face turns bright red from extreme embarrassment.

> Literally, "fire comes out of the face." This idiom comes from describing a very red—and embarrassed—face. We might associate flames with anger, but this idiom means to be "embarrassed."

EXAMPLE SENTENCE:

たくさんの<ruby>人前<rt>ひとまえ</rt></ruby>で<ruby>転<rt>ころ</rt></ruby>んでしまい、<ruby>顔<rt>かお</rt></ruby>から<ruby>火<rt>ひ</rt></ruby>が<ruby>出<rt>で</rt></ruby>た。

takusan no hitomae de koronde shimai, kao kara hi ga deta.

I tripped and fell in front of a lot of people and my face turned bright red (in embarrassment).

Example Sentence

VOCABULARY:

たくさん *takusan*—many

の *no*—of [modifying particle which connects a modifying word and word that is modified]

VOCABULARY

Learn Useful Words, Phrases, and Sayings

Vocabulary Continued

人前で *hitomae de*—in front of people; in the public; in the presence of people [人前 (presence of people; public) + で (in (front of))]

転んで *koronde*—to fall down; to take a fall [*te*-form of 転ぶ；this word implies falling down flat on the ground; *te*-form to connect the following word しまい]

しまい *shimai*—unfortunately (fell) and…; ended up (falling) [*masu*-stem of しまう；indicates unfortunate/unfavorable; *masu*-stem; functioning as a conjunctive]

顔 *kao*—face

から *kara*—from

火 *hi*— fire; flame

が *ga*—(marks what came out)

出た *deta*—came out [plain past form of 出る (to come out)]

顔から火が出た *kao kara hi ga deta*—face turned bright red (in embarrassment)

<ruby>神奈川<rt>か な が わ</rt></ruby>

Kanagawa 神奈川

Japanese: 神奈川県 *kanagawa ken*

Capital: 横浜 Yokohama

Population: 9,221,129 (April 1, 2022)

DID YOU KNOW?

As the second largest prefecture by population, Kanagawa is part of the Greater Tokyo Area. Commodore Perry landed in Kanagawa in 1853 which led to the opening of Japanese ports to the United States. To the right is The Great Wave off Kanagawa by ukiyoe artist Katsushika Hokusai.

PLACES TO SEE:

- **Kamakura**—once the political center of Japan, Kamakura houses numerous historical points of interest such as one of Japan's Great Buddhas.

- **Hakone**—with a view of Mt. Fuji, Hakone has hot springs, gardens, and Lake Ashinoko, a lake formed by Mount Hakone's last eruption 3,000 years ago.

- **Hakone Botanical Garden of Wetlands**—founded in 1976, the garden has over 1,700 varieties of plants native to Japan.

- **Yokohama**—Japan's second largest city with over three million residents.

- **Zoorasia**—a large zoo in Yokohama.

- **Hakkeijima Sea Paradise**—an aquatic amusement park and aquarium.

- **Doraemon Musuem**—houses an extensive collection of the work of Fujiko F. Fujio, the creator of Doraemon. Doraemon is a robot cat from the 22nd century.

FAMOUS FOR:

- **Population**—a relatively small prefecture, but is the second most populous prefecture in Japan.

- **Metropolitan Size**—Yokohama is the second largest city in Japan.

- **Yokohama Chinatown**—the largest in Japan.

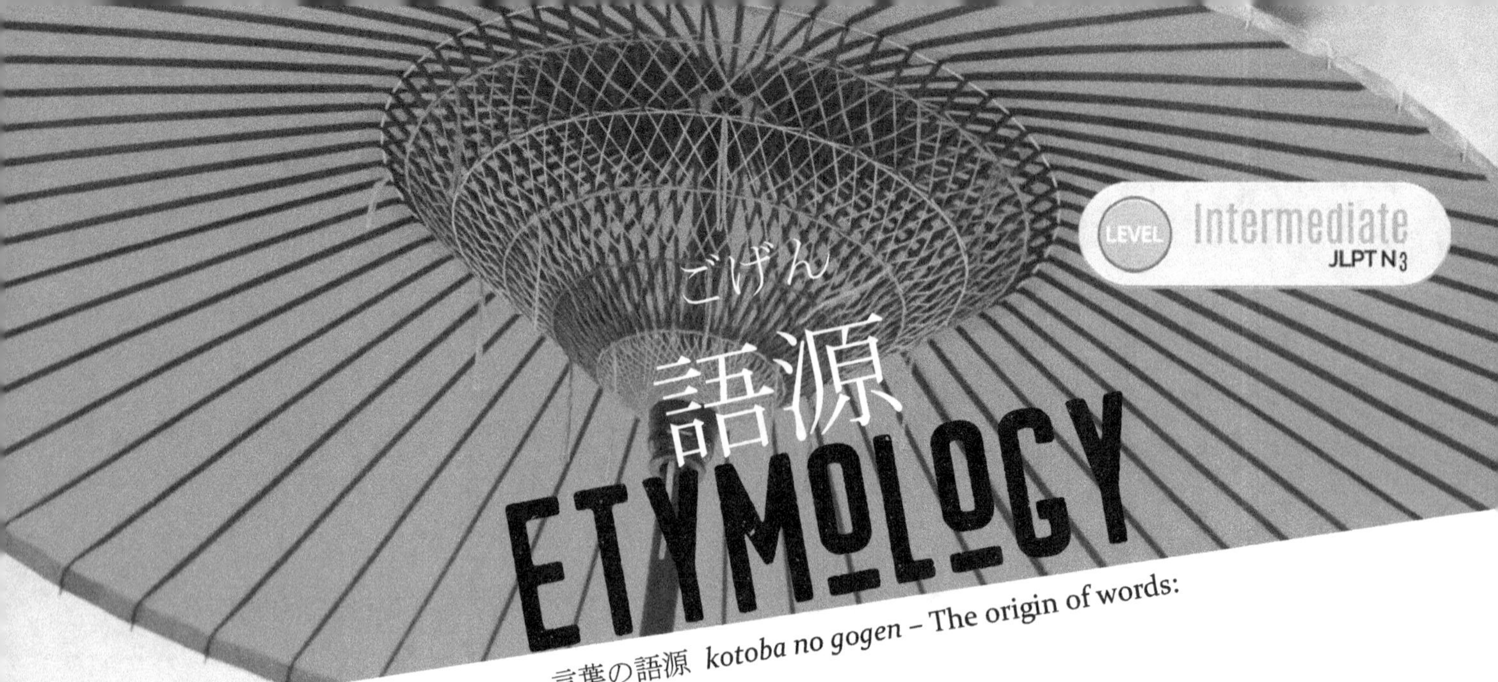

王国と帝国の違い

おうこく　　　ていこく　　　ちが

The difference between a Kingdom and an Empire

Scan for Recording

今回は、語源ではなく、王国と帝国の違いについて説明します。王国は、王様が治める国のことです。帝国は、こういった王国をいくつも持っている国のことで、皇帝が治めています。つまり、王様より皇帝のほうが偉いのです。

This time around, we will discuss the difference between a kingdom and an empire, instead of the etymology of a word.

A kingdom is a country ruled by a king. An empire has several such kingdoms and is ruled by an emperor. In other words, the emperor is greater than the king.

10

Vocabulary Continued

Vocabulary

語源 etymology; origin of a word

今回は this time; now [今回 (this time; now) + は (adds emphasis)]

語源ではなく instead of the etymology of a word [語源 (origin of a word; derivation of a word; etymology) + ではなく (instead of …; not …, but; as opposed to …)]

王国と帝国の違い the difference between a kingdom and an empire [王国 (kingdom; monarchy) + と (and) + 帝国 (empire) + の (modifier) + 違い (difference; distinction; discrepancy)]

について about; concerning; regarding

説明します discuss; explain; describe; expound; provide an explanation

王国は as for a kingdom [王国 (kingdom; monarchy) + は (indicates the sentence topic)]

王様が治める国 a country ruled by a king [王様 (king) + が (emphasizes the preceding word; identifies who performs the action) + 治める (to govern; to manage; to rule) + 国 (country; state)]

のこと all the things about (a country ruled by a king) [it has a "focusing" feature and lets you know that the subject has a certain quality; how to form: Noun + のこと]

です be; is

帝国は as for an empire [帝国 (empire) + は (indicates the sentence topic)]

こういった this sort of; this type of; such

王国をいくつも持っている国 a country that has several (such) kingdoms [王国 (kingdom; monarchy) + を (indicates the direct object of action) + いくつも (many; much; plenty; several) + 持っている (has; ている form of 持つ (to possess; to have) which is used to describe the actual state or condition of the subject) + 国 (country; state)]

のことで all the things about (a country that has several (such) kingdoms), and [のこと (all the things about) + で (て-form of です (be; is) which is used to connect to the next phrase, creating the meaning of "and")]

皇帝が治めています is ruled by an emperor; an emperor governs (a country) [皇帝 (emperor) + が (identifies who performs the action; emphasizes the preceding word) + 治めています (ています form of 治める (to govern; to rule) which is used to describe the actual state or condition of the subject)]

つまり that is to say; that is; in other words

王様より皇帝のほうが偉い the emperor is greater than the king [王様 (king) + より (than) + 皇帝 (emperor) + のほうが (conveys the idea that the noun it follows is "better" or "worse", "more" or "less", etc., depending on the sentence context) + 偉い (great; excellent; admirable; remarkable; distinguished); how to form: Noun-1 より + Noun-2 のほうが + Adjective]

のです the fact is that ...; it is that ...; the explanation is that ... [is used to explain something; shows emphasis]

ANIME / MANGA PHRASE

Surprise your Japanese friends with these phrases

Please see the sound files for the pronunciation

Scan for Recording

「もう大丈夫。なぜって？私が来た。」

オールマイトのセリフ

アニメ「僕のヒーローアカデミア」より

「mou daijoubu. naze tte? watashi ga kita.」

ooru maito no serifu

anime 「boku no hiiroo akademia」 yori

"Fear not. Why? I'm here."
Line of All Might
From the anime "My Hero Academia"

VOCABULARY

「」—(quotation marks; " ")

もう大丈夫 *mou daijoubu*—it's okay; fear not; it's all right now [もう (now; presently) + 大丈夫 (all right; alright; OK; okay)]

ANIME / MANGA PHRASE

Surprise your Japanese friends with these phrases

Vocabulary Continued

なぜって *naze tte*—why [なぜ (why) + って (a quotation marker (added to elicit further information))]

私が来た *watashi ga kita*—I'm here; I came [私 (I; me) + が (identifies who performs the action) + 来た (plain past form of 来る (to come; to arrive))]

オールマイトのセリフ *ooru maito no serifu*—Line of All Might [オールマイト (All Might) + の (of; 's; modifier) + セリフ (one's lines; speech; words)]

アニメ *anime*—anime; animation; animated film; animated cartoon

「僕のヒーローアカデミア」 *boku no hiiroo akademia* —"My Hero Academia" [「」 (quotation marks; " ") + 僕の (my; 僕 (I; me; male term or language) + の (indicates possessive)) + ヒーロー (hero) + アカデミア (academia)]

より *yori*—from

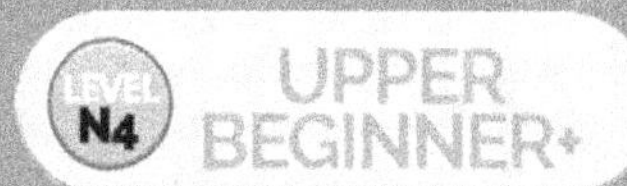

Matsuo Bashou 松尾芭蕉
_{まつおばしょう}

やがて死ぬ　景色は見えず

蝉の声

Haiku Audio

yagate shinu / keshiki wa miezu / semi no koe

They will soon die | but they don't appear so | the hardy trilling of cicadas

Explanation:

もうすぐ死んでしまう蝉なのに、死にそうな様子は見えない。一生懸命に鳴いています。

Explanation

Cicadas die soon, and yet they don't look to be dying. They are chirping with great enthusiasm.

Continued

Vocabulary

やがて before long; soon; shortly; in due time; in the course of time

死ぬ to die; to pass away

景色 scenery; sight; view; appearance [In this case, this refers to the appearance of the cicadas. They don't appear to be dying due to their loud voices, but they will soon all die nonetheless.]

は (indicates the sentence topic)

見えず (they) don't appear (to be dying) [from 見える (to look; to seem; to appear); ~ず means "without doing ~"; how to form: Verb (ない stem) + ず]

蝉の声 chirping of cicadas [蝉 (cicada; locust) + の (of; 's; modifier) + 声 (singing (of a bird); chirping (of an insect); voice)]

松尾芭蕉 Matsuo Bashou (1644-1694) [was the most famous poet of the Edo period in Japan and is recognized as the greatest master of haiku]

もうすぐ soon; shortly; before long; nearly; almost

死んでしまう蝉なのに cicadas die soon, and yet [死んでしまう (die; ~しまう refers to a regrettable event or negative meaning; how to form: Verb (て form) + しまう) + 蝉 (cicada; locust) + なのに (although; despite; even though; and yet; how to form: Noun + な + のに)]

死にそうな様子は見えない (they) don't look to be dying [死にそうな (dying; at the point of death; about to die; almost dead) + 様子 (appearance; look) + は (indicates the sentence

Vocabulary Continued

topic) + 見えない (don't look; plain negative form of 見える (to look; to seem; to appear))]

一生懸命に with all one's strength; with great enthusiasm; heartily; with heart and soul

鳴いています is/are chirping [ています-form of 鳴く (to make sound (of an animal); to sing; to chirp) which is used to express an ongoing action]

No matter how short of a time you have, give everything your best.

KANJI SPOTLIGHT

Learning kanji one character at a time.

JLPT N5 Kanji

月

On: **ガツ；ゲツ**

Kun: **つき**

Meaning: moon; month

Hint: This is a sun (日) with legs–the moon runs faster around the earth. Therefore it needs legs.

Audio of Readings

Stroke Order:

月 丿 刀 月 月

Examples:

いちがつ
一月 January [lit. 1st month]

こんげつ
今月 this month

つき
月 the moon

げつようび
月曜日 Monday

Audio of Example

きょう　　げつようび
今日は月曜日です。

kyou wa getsuyoubi desu.

Today is Monday.

[All the days of the week end with *~youbi*.]

VOCABULARY:

今日 *kyou*—today; this day

は *wa*—(indicates the sentence topic)

月曜日 *getsuyoubi*—Monday

です *desu*—be; is

の AS A PRONOUN

ABOUT:

You are probably aware of の as a possessive or limiting marker. の can also be used as a pronoun. In this case, it could be translated as "one."

HOW TO USE:

■ When the context is understood, replace the noun with の.

EXAMPLES:

赤いのが欲しいです。

I want the red **one**.

[red | one | want]

先週見たのを買った。

I bought the **one** (I) saw last week.

[last week | saw | one | bought]

Example 1

Example 2

19

Continued

VOCABULARY:

赤い *akai*—red; crimson; scarlet

の *no*—one [is used as a pronoun]

が *ga*—(indicates the object of emotion)

欲しい *hoshii*—wanting (to have); desiring; wishing for

です *desu*—be; is

先週 *senshuu*—last week; the week before

見た *mita*—saw [plain past form of 見る (to see; to look; to watch; to view)]

を *o*—(indicates the direct object of action)

買った *katta*—bought [plain past form of 買う (to buy; to purchase)]

よんでみよう！LET'S READ!

Learn through reading for (very) beginners of Japanese

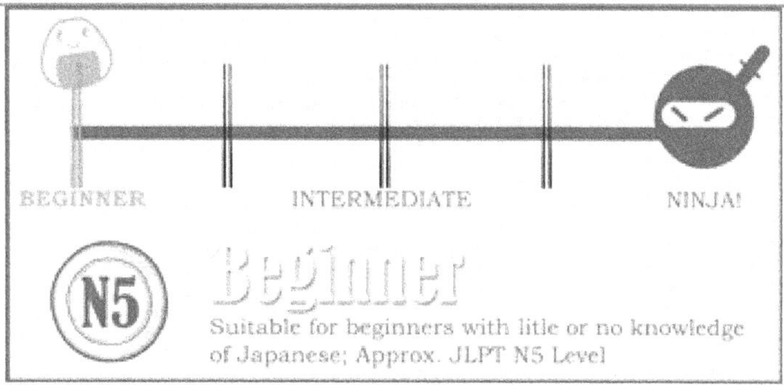

Have you only recently learned hiragana but need practice? Or perhaps, your hiragana is no problem, but you want to build your reading comprehension?

This segment is here to the rescue!

Read real Japanese—beginner level but not boring Japanese! Enjoy reading flash fiction, super short essays, and funny stories of common mistakes made by foreigners in Japan.

Best of all, the only requirement is that you can read hiragana. Vocabulary and grammar will be defined and explained.

The format is a little different from our other more advanced readers. The idea is for the reader to read the entire story three times. Each page will have a sentence or two in hiragana (with spaces between words for you to see "words" instead of syllables) at the top and that same content in full Japanese (with furigana) at the bottom. The middle will have the glossary and grammatical explanations. Lastly, the story will be presented in Japanese without furigana. See if you can read it after going through the explanations.

If you have just learned hiragana, you may want to listen to the sound file while reading the hiragana section to practice correct pronunciation. If you have studied Japanese a bit longer, you may want to start with the bottom version and take note of the glossary for understanding.

Makoto+ members can access this in a more interactive format. To learn more:

http://MakotoPlus.com

And now...

Let's learn about...

COLD MEALS

Normal Speed

Slow Speed

The top and bottom Japanese texts are identical in meaning. The top version is only in hiragana and includes spaces between words. The bottom version has no spaces and uses kanji with furigana. Unless you are just practicing hiragana recognition, try to work through both versions. Scan the QR codes for the sound files.

Normal Speed

Slow Speed

冷(つめ)たい食事(しょくじ)

COLD MEALS

あめりか　や　よーろっぱ　で　は、つめたい　しょくじ　は　あまり　たべません。つめたい　もの　は、　おいしくない　と　おもわれて　います。

GLOSSARY AND NOTES

アメリカやヨーロッパ *amerika ya yo-roppa*—United States and Europe [アメリカ (America; United States; US; USA) + や (and) + ヨーロッパ (Europe)]

では *de wa*—in [で (in; at; indicates the location of action) + は (adds emphasis)]

冷たい食事 *tsumetai shokuji*—cold meals [冷(つめ)たい (cold (to the touch); chilly; icy; freezing) + 食事(しょくじ) (meal)]

は *wa*—(indicates the sentence topic)

あまり食べません *amari tabemasen*—is/are not eaten very often; not eat very much [from 食(た)べる (to eat); あまり~ない means "not very; not much ~"; how to form: あまり + Verb (negative form)]

冷たいもの *tsumetai mono*—cold food; cold meal [冷(つめ)たい (cold) + もの (substance; thing)]

おいしくない *oishikunai*—not tasty [plain negative form of おいしい (good(-tasting); nice; delicious; tasty)]

と思われています *to omowarete imasu*—is/are considered [と (used for quoting (thoughts, speech, etc.)) + 思(おも)われています (ています-form of 思(おも)われる (plain passive form of 思(おも)う (to think; to consider; to believe)) which is used to describe the actual state or condition of the subject)]

アメリカやヨーロッパでは、冷(つめ)たい食事(しょくじ)はあまり食(た)べません。

冷(つめ)たいものは、おいしくないと思(おも)われています。

でも、にほん　で　は　なつ　に　なる　と、うどん　や　そば　など
を　つめたく　して　たべます。

GLOSSARY AND NOTES

でも　*demo*—but; however

日本では　*nihon de wa*—in Japan [日本 (Japan) + では (in)]

夏になると　*natsu ni naru to*—in summer; with the arrival of summer; come summer [夏 (summer) + になると (when it becomes; when it comes to; になる (come to; become; turn out) + と (if; when))]

うどんやそば　*udon ya soba*—*udon* and *soba* [うどん (*udon*; thick Japanese wheat noodles) + や (and; such things as …) + そば (*soba*; Japanese buckwheat noodles)]

など　*nado*—et cetera; etc.; and the like; and so forth

を　*o*—(indicates the direct object of action)

冷たくして食べます　*tsumetaku shite tabemasu*—eat (it) cold; make (it) cold and eat [冷たくして (make it cold; て-form of 冷たくする (from 冷たい (cold (to the touch); chilly; icy); ~くする means "to make something whatever the adjective describes"; how to form: い-adjective い + くする) which is used to connect to the next verb) + 食べます (eat)]

でも、日本では夏になると、うどんやそばなどを冷たくして食べます。

にほん　の　なつ　は、とても　むしあつく、つめたい　もの　の　ほ
う　が　たべやすい　から　です。つめたい　そうめん　など　は　と
ても　おいしい　です　ね。

GLOSSARY AND NOTES

日本の夏　*nihon no natsu*—summer in Japan [日本 (Japan) + の (of; 's; in; modifier) + 夏 (summer)]

とても　*totemo*—very

蒸し暑く　*mushiatsuku*—hot and humid, and [adverbial form of 蒸し暑い (hot and humid; steaming hot; sultry) which is used to connect to the next phrase, creating the meaning of "and"]

冷たいもののほうが食べやすい　*tsumetai mono no hou ga tabeyasui*—cold food is easier to eat [冷たい (cold (to the touch)) + もの (substance) + のほうが (conveys the idea that the noun it follows is "better" or "worse", "more" or "less", etc., depending on the sentence context) + 食べやすい (easy to eat; from 食べる (to eat); ~やすい means "easy to; likely to; prone to"; how to form: Verb (ます-stem form) + やすい)]

から　*kara*—because; since

です　*desu*—be; is

冷たいそうめん　*tsumetai soumen*—cold *soumen* [冷たい (cold) + そうめん (*soumen*; fine white noodles)]

とてもおいしい　*totemo oishii*—taste very great; very tasty [とても (very; exceedingly) + おいしい (good(-tasting); nice; delicious; tasty)]

ね　*ne*—(sentence ender) [is used to express your opinion]

日本の夏は、とても蒸し暑く、冷たいもののほうが食べやすい

からです。冷たいそうめんなどはとてもおいしいですね。

冷たい食事

COLD MEALS

Now, let's read the story once more in natural Japanese.
Lastly, check the English translation to make sure you understand.

アメリカやヨーロッパでは、冷たい食事はあまり食べません。冷たいものは、おいしくないと思われています。でも、日本では夏になると、うどんやそばなどを冷たくして食べます。日本の夏は、とても蒸し暑く、冷たいもののほうが食べやすいからです。冷たいそうめんなどはとてもおいしいですね。

ENGLISH: (try to save this for last)

In the United States and Europe, cold meals are not eaten very often. Cold foods are considered not tasty. However, in Japan, people eat *udon* and *soba* noodles cold in the summer. This is because summer in Japan is very hot and humid, and cold food is easier to eat. Cold *soumen* noodles tastes very great.

<table>
<tr><td colspan="2" align="center">KEY VOCABULARY</td></tr>
</table>

冷たい食事 *tsumetai shokuji*—cold meals [冷たい (cold (to the touch); chilly; freezing) + 食事 (meal)]	(and; such things as ...) + そば (*soba*; Japanese buckwheat noodles)]
アメリカやヨーロッパ *amerika ya yo-roppa*—United States and Europe [アメリカ (America; USA) + や (and) + ヨーロッパ (Europe)]	蒸し暑い *mushiatsui*—hot and humid; steaming hot; sultry)
おいしくない *oishikunai*—not tasty	冷たいそうめん *tsumetai soumen*—cold *soumen* [冷たい (cold) + そうめん (*soumen*; fine white noodles)]
夏 *natsu*—summer	
うどんやそば *udon ya soba*—*udon* and *soba* [うどん (*udon*; thick Japanese wheat noodles) + や	とてもおいしい *totemo oishii*—taste very great; very tasty [とても (very; exceedingly) + おいしい (good(-tasting); nice; delicious; tasty)]

JAPANESE READER

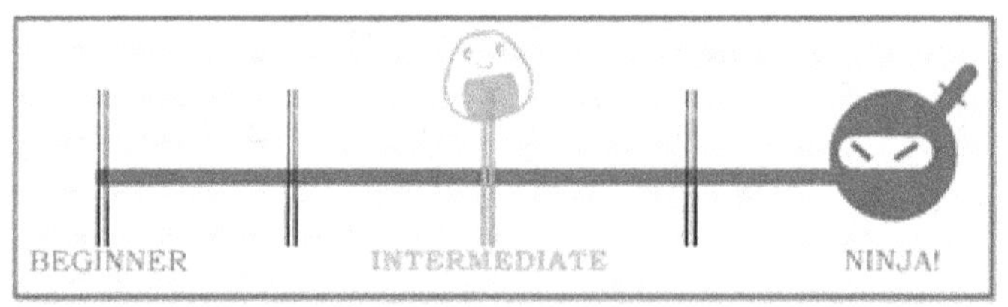

れ き し
アニメの歴史
History of Animation

Story Read Normal

Story Read Slow Speed

Tezuka Osamu in 1951

https://en.wikipedia.org/wiki/Osamu_Tezuka#/media/File:Osamu_Tezuka_1951_Scan10008-2.JPG

Work through the story, sentence-by-sentence, referring to the vocabulary and grammar explanations below as needed.

日本のアニメは、世界中で人気があります。日本語を勉強する

きっかけがアニメだったという人も多いでしょう。

アニメの歴史 history of animation [アニメ (animation; animated film; animated cartoon; anime) + の (of; 's; modifier) + 歴史 (history)]

日本のアニメ Japanese anime [日本 (Japan) + の (of; modifier) + アニメ (anime; animation)]

は (indicates the sentence topic)

世界中で all over the world [世界中 (around the world; throughout the world) + で (indicates a total or an extent)]

人気があります be liked by everybody; popular; star; enjoy popularity; be well thought of

日本語を勉強するきっかけがアニメだった (it) was anime that inspired (them) to study the Japanese lan-guage [日本語 (Japanese (language)) + を (indicates the direct object of action) + 勉強する (to study) + きっかけ (inspire; trigger) + が (emphasizes the preceding word) + アニメ (anime) + だった (was; plain past form of です (be; is))]

という人も多いでしょう many people may say that [という (that; that says) + 人 (people) + も (emphasizes the preceding word) + 多い (many; numerous; a lot) + でしょう (may; it seems; I think; I guess)]

さて、その日本のアニメはいつどのように始まってどのように発展したのでしょうか？１９１７年（大正６年）に日本で初めてアニメーション映画が製作されました。

さて　now then; and now; well

その日本のアニメは that Japanese animation [その (that; the) + 日本のアニメ (Japanese animation) + は (indicates the sentence topic)]

いつ　when; at what time

どのように　how; in what way

始まって begin and [て-form of 始まる (to begin; to start) which is used to connect to the next phrase, creating the meaning of "and"]

どのように発展した how did it develop? [どのように (how; in what way) + 発展した (developed; plain past form of 発展する (to develop; to evolve))]

のでしょうか (ask a question in a polite way)

1917年（大正6年）に in 1917 (Taishou 6) [年 (year) + 大正 (Taishou era (1912.7.30-1926.12.25)) + に (in (time))]

日本で in Japan [日本 (Japan) + で (in; indicates the location of action)]

初めて for the first time

アニメーション映画が製作されました animated film was produced [アニメーション映画 (animated film; animated movie; an animated feature film) + が (emphasizes the preceding word) + 製作されました (was produced; polite past form of 製作される (plain passive form of 製作する (to produce)))]

当時、外国で製作された短編のアニメーション映画がとても人気

があったので、日本でも作ってみようという事になったようで

す。しかし、たいへん小さなスタジオで少人数で製作していま

した。

当時 around that time; at that time; back in those days; at that point in time

外国で製作された produced in other countries [外国 (foreign country; other countries; another country; overseas) + で (in; indicates the location of action) + 製作された (produced; plain past form of 製作される (plain passive form of 製作する (to produce)))]

短編のアニメーション映画が short animated films [短編 (short (e.g. story, film)) + の (modifier) + アニメーション映画 (animated film) + が (emphasizes the preceding word)]

とても人気があった was/were very popular [とても (very; exceedingly) + 人気があった (was/were popular)]

ので so; because of …; the reason is …

日本でも in Japan as well [日本 (Japan) + で (in) + も (too; also; as well)]

作ってみようという事になったようです (they) decided to try making (them) [作ってみよう (try making; from 作る (to make; to produce); ~てみよう is the plain

volitional form of ~てみる (to give something a try to see how it goes; how to form: Verb て-form + みる); volitional form is used when making a suggestion to one or more people including oneself) + という (is used to define, describe, and generally just talk about the thing itself) + 事になった (decided; plain past form of 事になる (it has been decided that..; it turns out that..; how to form: Verb (dictionary form) + 事になる)) + ようです (indicates how something would seem based on our judgment and any evidence)]

しかし however; but

たいへん小さなスタジオで少人数で製作していました it was produced by a small number of people in a very small studio [たいへん (very) + 小さな (small; little; tiny) + スタジオ (studio) + で (in; indicates the location of action) + 少人数 (small number of people) + で (by; indicates means of action) + 製作していました (was produced; ていました form (past continuous form) of 製作する (to produce) which places focus on the duration of a past action)]

せんきゅうひゃくごじゅうさんねん　　　　　　　　　ほうそう　　　はじ

１　９　５　３年にテレビ放送が始まりましたが、アニメは、

せいさく　　　　　　　　　じかん　　　かね　　　　　　　　　　　　　　　　　　ほんかくてき

製作するのに時間とお金がかかるため、なかなか本格的にアニメ

ひと　　　あらわ

をつくろうとする人が現れませんでした。

１９53年に in 1953 [年 (year) + に (in; specifies time)]

テレビ放送が始まりました television broadcasting began [テレビ (television; TV) + 放送 (broadcasting; broadcast; program; announcement) + が (emphasizes the preceding word; identifies what performs the action) + 始まりました (began; polite past form of 始まる (to begin; to start))]

が but; however

製作するのに時間とお金がかかる (it) takes time and money to produce (animation) [製作する (to produce) + のに (to (do something); in order to ~; how to form: Verb (dictionary form) + のに) + 時間 (time) + と (and) + お金 (money) + が (emphasizes the preceding word) + かかる (to take (a resource))]

ため because; for

なかなか by no means; not readily; difficult to

本格的に in earnest; at full scale; for real

なかなか本格的にアニメをつくろうとする人が現れませんでした it was difficult to find people who tried to create animation in earnest [なかなか (difficult) + 本格的に (in earnest) + アニメ (animation) + を (indicates the direct object of action) + つくろうとする (to try to create; 「Verb volitional form + とする」 means "to try to do ~; to be about to do ~") + 人 (person; people) + が (emphasizes the preceding word) + 現れませんでした (did not appear; polite negative past form of 現れる (to appear; to come in sight; to become visible; to come out)); なかなか~ない means "not easy to; difficult to; struggling to; can't seem to~"; how to form: なかなか ~ Verb (negative form)]

<ruby>海外<rt>かいがい</rt></ruby>から<ruby>輸入<rt>ゆにゅう</rt></ruby>されたアニメを<ruby>放送<rt>ほうそう</rt></ruby>していました。

<ruby>１９６３年<rt>せんきゅうひゃくろくじゅうさんねん</rt></ruby>、<ruby>手塚治虫<rt>てづかおさむ</rt></ruby>が<ruby>作<rt>つく</rt></ruby>った「<ruby>虫<rt>むし</rt></ruby>プロダクション」は、<ruby>日本初<rt>にほんはつ</rt></ruby>の<ruby>本格的<rt>ほんかくてき</rt></ruby>なアニメ「<ruby>鉄腕<rt>てつわん</rt></ruby>アトム」を<ruby>製作<rt>せいさく</rt></ruby>して、<ruby>放送<rt>ほうそう</rt></ruby>しました。

海外から from abroad [海外 (abroad; foreign; overseas) + から (from)]

輸入されたアニメを放送していました animations imported (from abroad) were broadcasted [輸入された (imported; plain passive past form of 輸入する (to import; to buy from foreign countries)) + アニメ (animation; animated film; animated cartoon; anime) + を (indicates the direct object of action) + 放送していました (were broadcasted; ていました form (past continuous form) of 放送する (do a broadcast; transmit; air) which places focus on the duration of a past action)]

１９６３年 in 1963 [年 (year)]

手塚治虫が作った created by Tezuka Osamu [手塚治虫 (Tezuka Osamu) + が (identifies who performs the action) + 作った (created; plain past form of 作る (to create; to make))]

「虫プロダクション」 "Mushi Productions" [「」 (quotation marks; " ") + 虫 (Mushi) + プロダクション (Production)]

日本初の本格的なアニメ「鉄腕アトム」を製作して produced Japan's first full-scale animation "Astro Boy" [日本 (Japan) + 初 (first; new) + の ('s; of; modifier) + 本格的な (full-scale; all-out; real; earnest) + アニメ (animation) + 「鉄腕アトム」 ("Astro Boy") + を (indicates the direct object of action) + 製作して (て-form of 製作する (to produce) which is used to connect to the next phrase)]

放送しました was/were broadcasted [polite past form of 放送する (to broadcast; to air; to transmit)]

その後、タツノコプロが「マッハゴーゴーゴー」を制作しまし

た。７０年代にはロボットのアニメが子供たちの間でたいへ

ん人気になりました。アニメに登場するロボットのおもちゃが

売り出され、こちらも売り上げを伸ばしました。

その後 later; after that time; subsequent to that; afterward [その (that; the) + 後 (after; later)]

タツノコプロが「マッハゴーゴーゴー」を制作しました Tatsunoko Production produced "Mach Go Go Go (Speed Racer)" [タツノコプロ (Tatsunoko Production) + が (emphasizes the preceding word; identifies what performs the action) + 「マッハゴーゴーゴー」 ("Mach Go Go Go (Speed Racer)") + を (indicates the direct object of action) + 制作しました (produced; polite past form of 制作する (to produce; to make))]

70年代には in the 1970s [70年代 (1970s; 年代 (age; era; period)) + には (in; puts more emphasis and restriction on the preceding word)]

ロボットのアニメが robot-themed anime [ロボット (robot) + の (of; modifier) + アニメ (anime) + が (emphasizes the preceding word)]

子供たちの間で among children [子供たち (children; たち is a pluralizing suffix especially for people and animals) + の間で (among; by and between)]

たいへん人気になりました became very popular [たいへん (very; greatly) + 人気 (popularity; public favor) + になりました (became; polite past form of なる (become; turn out; come to))]

アニメに登場するロボットのおもちゃが toys of the robots that appeared in the anime [アニメ (anime) + の (modifier) + 登場する (make one's appearance; enter into the picture; at play; appear; hit the scene) + ロボット (robot) + の (of) + おもちゃ (toy) + が (emphasizes the preceding word)]

売り出され (toys) were marketed, and [ます-stem form of 売り出されます (polite passive positive form of 売り出す (to put on the market; to put out for sale; to begin selling; to market)) which is used to connect to the next phrase, creating the meaning of "and"]

こちらも these (toys) also [こちら (these; this (one)) + も (too; also)]

売り上げを伸ばしました made the sales go up; sales (of toys) increased [polite past form of 売り上げを伸ばす (get increased sales; extend sales; build sales; pump up sale)]

８０年代に入ると、「ドラゴンボール」「北斗の拳」なども

人気になりました。８０年代後半には、宮崎駿監督が「とな

りのトトロ」「天空の城ラピュタ」などを発表しました。

80年代に入ると in the 1980s [80 年代 (1980s; 年代 (age; era; period)) + に (in; specifies time) + 入る (to enter; to go into) + と (if; when)]

「ドラゴンボール」 "Dragon Ball" [「」 (quotation marks; " ") + ドラゴン (dragon) + ボール (ball)]

「北斗の拳」 "Fist of the North Star" [「」 (quotation marks; " ") + 北斗 (the Big Dipper (asterism)) + の (of) + 拳 (fist)]

など et cetera; etc.; and the like; and so forth

も too; also; as well

人気になりました became popular [人気 (popularity; public favor) + に (expresses the result of change) + なりました (became; polite past form of なる (to become; to turn out; to attain))]

80年代後半には in the late '80s [80年代 ('80s; 年代 (age; era; period)) + 後半 (second half; latter half; latter part; late) + に (in; specifies time) + は (adds emphasis)]

宮崎駿監督が director Miyazaki Hayao [宮崎駿 (Miyazaki Hayao) + 監督 (director) + が (emphasizes the preceding word)]

「となりのトトロ」「天空の城ラピュタ」などを発表しました released "My Neighbor Totoro", "Laputa: Castle in the Sky", etc. [「となりのトトロ」 ("My Neighbor Totoro"; となり (next-door neighbor; next (to); adjoining; adjacent) + の (modifier) + トトロ (Totoro)) + 「天空の城ラピュタ」 ("Laputa: Castle in the Sky"; 天空 (sky; air; ether; firmament; the heavens) + の (in; of; modifier) + 城 (castle) + ラピュタ (Laputa)) + など (et cetera; etc.; and the like; and so forth) + を (indicates the direct object of action) + 発表しました (released; polite past form of 発表する (release; publish; introduce; set out; go public))]

９０年代「エバンゲリオン」「攻殻機動隊」「ポケモン」な

どがヒットしました。今でも人気があります。2000年代になる

と、「ナルト」が登場しました。これは、アメリカで放映され

て大ヒットしました。

90年代 in the 1990s [年代 (age; era; period)]

「エバンゲリオン」「攻殻機動隊」「ポケモン」など
がヒットしました "Evangelion", "Ghost in the Shell",
"Pokemon", etc. became a hit [「エバンゲリオン」
("Evangelion") + 「攻殻機動隊」("Ghost in the Shell") +
「ポケモン」("Pokemon") + など (et cetera; etc.; and
the like; and so forth) + が (identifies what performs
the action) + ヒットしました (became a hit; polite past
form of ヒットする (become a hit; win a big market))]

今でも人気があります still popular today [今 (now; the
present time) + でも (still; yet; also; as well) + 人気があ
ります (popular; be liked by everybody; star; enjoy
popularity)]

2000年代になると in the 2000s [2000 年代 (2000s; 年代
(age; era; period)) + になると (in; expresses the meaning "in this period"; how to form: Noun + になると)]

「ナルト」が登場しました "Naruto" appeared [「ナル
ト」("Naruto") + が (identifies what performs the action; emphasizes the preceding word) + 登場しました

(appeared; polite past form of 登場する (appear; at
play; come on stage; hit the scene))]

これは it [これ (it; this; this one) + は (indicates the
sentence topic)]

アメリカで in the United States [アメリカ (America;
United States; US; USA) + で (in; indicates the location of action)]

放映されて (it) was broadcasted and [て-form of 放映
される (plain passive form of 放映する(broadcast;
air; show)) which is used to connect to the next
phrase, creating the meaning of "and"]

大ヒットしました became a big hit [大 (big; great;
huge) + ヒットしました (became a hit)]

みやざきはやおかんとく　せん　ちひろ　かみかく　せかいてき

また、宮崎駿監督の「千と千尋の神隠し」が世界的にヒットし

しょう　じゅしょう　さいきん

て、アメリカのアカデミー賞も受賞しました。そして、最近の

だい　きめつ　やいば

大ヒットは、なんといっても「鬼滅の刃」。

また also; as well; likewise

宮崎駿監督の「千と千尋の神隠し」 "Spirited Away"
directed by Miyazaki Hayao; "Spirited Away" of director Miyazaki Hayao [宮崎駿 (Miyazaki Hayao) +
監督 (director) + の (of; 's; modifier) + 「千と千尋の
神隠し」 ("Spirited Away")]

世界的にヒットして became a worldwide hit and [
世界的に (worldwide) + ヒットして (became a hit
and; て-form of ヒットする (become a hit) which is
used to connect to the next phrase, creating the
meaning of "and")]

アメリカのアカデミー賞も受賞しました won an
Academy Award in the United States [アメリカ
(United States; America; USA) + の (in; of; modifier)
+ アカデミー賞 (Academy Award; アカデミー
(academy) + 賞 (award; prize)) + も (emphasizes

the preceding word) + 受賞しました (won a prize;
polite past form of 受賞する (win a prize; achieve
an award; receive a prize))]

そして and; and then

最近の大ヒットは the latest big hit [最近 (latest;
newly; recently; these days) + の (of; modifier) + 大
(big; great; huge) + ヒット (hit; success) + は
(indicates the sentence topic)]

なんといっても undeniably; after all is said and
done; no matter what people say

「鬼滅の刃」 "Demon Slayer" [「鬼滅の刃」
("Kimetsu no Yaiba (Demon Slayer)")]

私 も 見始めたら、止まらなくなってしまって、1シーズンを

たったの2日で見ました。日本のアニメは、ジャンルが幅広く

て、いろいろな楽しみ方ができます。

私も見始めたら when I also started watching (it) [私 (I; me) + も (also; too) + 見始めたら (when (I) started watching; from 見始める (to start to watch; to begin to watch; how to form: Verb (ます-stem form) + 始める); ~ら means "when; if"; how to form: Verb (た form) + ら)]

止まらなくなってしまって (I) couldn't stop and [from 止まらなくなる (can not stop; do not stop); ~てしまって is the て-form of ~てしまう (is used when you do things unintentionally; how to form: Verb て-form + しまう) which is used to connect to the next phrase, creating the meaning of "and"]

1シーズンをたったの2日で見ました watched the whole season in just two days [1シーズン (one season; the whole season) + を (indicates the direct object of action) + たった (only; merely; but; no more than) + の (modifier) + 2日 (two days; 日 (counter for days)) + で (in; indicates a total or an extent) + 見ました (watched; polite past form of 見る (to watch))]

ジャンルが幅広くて (Japanese anime) has a wide range of genres and [ジャンル (genre; category; kind) + が (emphasizes the preceding word) + 幅広くて (て-form of 幅広い (wide; broad; wide range of) which is used to connect to the next phrase, creating the meaning of "and"; how to form: remove the ~い ending from the い-adjective and replace it with く then add て)]

いろいろな楽しみ方ができます can be enjoyed in various ways [いろいろな (various; all sorts of; variety of) + 楽しみ方 (ways to enjoy; ways to have fun) + が (is used with potential form of a verb) + できます (can do; to be able to do; polite potential form of する (to do))]

ファンタジー、SF、学園もの、恋愛ものなど本当にたくさんあ
ります。コミックを原作にしたものもたくさんあります。最近
では登場人物になりきるコスプレも世界的に流行していま
す。

ファンタジー、SF、学園もの、恋愛もの fantasy,
science fiction, campus-life story, romance [ファン
タジー (fantasy) + SF (science fiction; sci-fi) + 学園
もの (campus-life story) + 恋愛もの (romance; love
story)]

など et cetera; etc.; and the like; and so forth

本当に really; truly

たくさんあります have many; there are so many of
them [たくさん (a lot; lots; plenty; many; much) +
あります (to have)]

コミックを原作にしたものもたくさんあります there
are also many based on comic books [コミック
(comic books; comics) + を (indicates the direct object of action) + 原作にした (based on) + もの
(thing; a generic noun which varies in meaning depending on the sentence context) + も (also; too; as
well) + たくさんあります (have many; there are
many)]

最近では recently [最近 (recently; lately; these days;
nowadays) + で (indicates time of action) + は
(adds emphasis)]

登場人物になりきるコスプレ cosplay, in which peo-
ple pretend to be the characters (in an anime) [
登場人物 (character (in a play or novel); dramatis
personae) + に (expresses the result of change) + な
りきる (to turn completely into; to become completely; act like; pretend to be) + コスプレ (cosplay
(dressing up as a character from an anime, manga,
video game, etc.); short for "costume play")]

も as well; also; too

世界的に流行しています has been popular worldwide [世界的に (worldwide; global) + 流行してい
ます (has been popular; ~しています-form of
流行する (become a fad; popular; become fash-
ionable) which is used to describe the actual condition of the subject; how to form: Verb て-form + い
ます)]

にほんじん　　　　　　　　　　　　　　　　　そだ　　　　　　　　　　　　　　いっしょうわす

日本人は、アニメとともに育っていますから、一生忘れられな

さくひん　　　　　　　　　　　　　　　　　　　　　じかい　　　　にほん

い作品というものもあります。さて、次回は、日本のアニメの

たてやくしゃ　　てづかおさむ　　　　　　　くわ　　　　つた　　　　　おも

立役者、手塚治虫について詳しくお伝えしたいと思います。お

たの

楽しみに！！

日本人 Japanese people; Japanese person

アニメとともに with anime [アニメ (anime) + ととも
に (with; at the same time as; together with); how to
form: Noun + とともに]

育っています has/have grown up; growing; grow [て
います-form of 育つ (to be brought up; to grow
(up)) which is used to describe an ongoing action]

から since; because

一生忘れられない作品というものもあります some
films also are unforgettable for the rest of (their)
lives [一生 (whole life; a lifetime; all through life) +
忘れられない (unforgettable; memorable) + 作品
(work (e.g. book, film, composition, etc.); opus; per-
formance) + という (that; is used to define, describe, and generally just talk about the thing itself)
+ もの (things; some; those) + も (also; too) + あり
ます (there is/are; to have)]

さて now; well; then

次回は in the next issue; next time around [次回 (next
time) + は (adds emphasis)]

日本のアニメの立役者 the driving force behind Japa-

nese animation [日本のアニメ (Japanese animation) + の (of; modifier) + 立役者 (driving force;
central figure; key figure; leading spirit)]

手塚治虫について about Tezuka Osamu [手塚治虫
(Tezuka Osamu) + について (about; regarding;
concerning)]

詳しくお伝えしたいと思います (I) would like to tell
(you) more; want to tell (you) in detail [詳しく (in
detail; fully; minutely; at full length) + お伝えした
い (would like to tell; from お伝えする (to tell; to
convey; to impart; お〜する allows one to speak
humbly of one's own actions; how to form: お +
Verb (ます-stem form) + する); 〜たい means
"want to do something"; how to form: Verb (ます-
stem form) + たい) + と (used for quoting
(thoughts, speech, etc.)) + 思います (to think (of
doing); to plan (to do); to consider)]

お楽しみに don't miss it; wait till; look forward to it

History of Animation

Please try to tackle the Japanese first and use this only as needed.

Japanese anime is popular all over the world. Many people may say that it was anime that inspired them to study the Japanese language. Now then, when did Japanese animation begin and how did it develop?

The first animated film was produced in Japan in 1917 (Taishou 6). Around that time, short animated films produced in other countries were very popular, so they decided to try making them in Japan as well. However, it was produced by a small number of people in a very small studio.

Television broadcasting began in 1953, but because of the time and money required to produce animation, it was difficult to find people who tried to create animation in earnest. Animations imported from abroad were broadcasted.

In 1963, "Mushi Productions" created by Tezuka Osamu, produced Japan's first full-scale animation "Astro Boy", which was broadcasted.

Later, Tatsunoko Production produced "Mach Go Go Go (Speed Racer)".

In the 1970s, robot-themed anime became very popular among children. Toys of the robots that appeared in the anime were marketed, and sales of these toys also increased.

In the 1980s, "Dragon Ball" and "Fist of the North Star" also became popular.

In the late '80s, director Miyazaki Hayao released "My Neighbor Totoro" and "Laputa: Castle in the Sky".

In the 1990s, "Evangelion", "Ghost in the Shell", and "Pokemon" became a hit. They are still popular today.

In the 2000s, "Naruto" appeared. It was broadcasted in the United States and became a big hit. Also, "Spirited Away" directed by Miyazaki Hayao became a worldwide hit and won an Academy Award in the United States.

And the latest big hit is, undeniably, "Kimetsu no Yaiba (Demon Slayer)". When I also started watching it, I couldn't stop and watched the whole season in just two days.

Japanese anime has a wide range of genres and can be enjoyed in various ways. Fantasy, science fiction, campus-life story, romance, and so many more. There are also many based on comic books.

Recently, cosplay, in which people pretend to be the characters in an anime, has been popular worldwide as well. Since Japanese people have grown up with anime, some films also are unforgettable for the rest of their lives.

Now, in the next issue, I would like to tell you more about Tezuka Osamu, the driving force behind Japanese animation. Don't miss it!!

アニメの歴史

　日本のアニメは、世界中で人気があります。日本語を勉強するきっかけがアニメだったという人も多いでしょう。さて、その日本のアニメはいつどのように始まってどのように発展したのでしょうか？

　1917年（大正6年）に日本で初めてアニメーション映画が製作されました。当時、外国で製作された短編のアニメーション映画がとても人気があったので、日本でも作ってみようという事になったようです。しかし、たいへん小さなスタジオで少人数で製作していました。

　１９５３年にテレビ放送が始まりましたが、アニメは、製作するのに時間とお金がかかるため、なかなか本格的にアニメをつくろうとする人が現れませんでした。海外から輸入されたアニメを放送していました。

　１９６３年、手塚治虫が作った「虫プロダクション」は、日本初の本格的なアニメ「鉄腕アトム」を製作して、放送しました。

　その後、タツノコプロが「マッハゴーゴーゴー」を制作しました。

　70年代にはロボットのアニメが子供たちの間でたいへん人気になりました。アニメに登場するロボットのおもちゃが売り出され、こちらも売り上げを伸ばしました。

　80年代に入ると、「ドラゴンボール」「北斗の拳」なども人気になりました。

Continued

　80年代後半には、宮崎駿監督が「となりのトトロ」「天空の城ラピュタ」などを発表しました。

　90年代「エバンゲリオン」「攻殻機動隊」「ポケモン」などがヒットしました。今でも人気があります。

　2000年代になると、「ナルト」が登場しました。これは、アメリカで放映されて大ヒットしました。また、宮崎駿監督の「千と千尋の神隠し」が世界的にヒットして、アメリカのアカデミー賞も受賞しました。

　そして、最近の大ヒットは、なんといっても「鬼滅の刃」。私も見始めたら、止まらなくなってしまって、1シーズンをたったの2日で見ました。

　日本のアニメは、ジャンルが幅広くて、いろいろな楽しみ方ができます。ファンタジー、SF、学園もの、恋愛ものなど本当にたくさんあります。コミックを原作にしたものもたくさんあります。

　最近では登場人物になりきるコスプレも世界的に流行しています。日本人は、アニメとともに育っていますから、一生忘れられない作品というものもあります。

　さて、次回は、日本のアニメの立役者、手塚治虫について詳しくお伝えしたいと思います。お楽しみに！！

Kanji in Focus

It is usually helpful to create a story based on the meanings of the kanji parts. Often, different kanji learning systems will use different "meanings" for the parts. We try to give the most common ones, but consistency is best. Choose one meaning per kanji part and stick with it. The following are a selection of the kanji found in this story. The <u>under-lined</u> reading is probably the most used.

歴	**READINGS** **MEANING** **EXAMPLE**	<u>レキ</u> curriculum; continuation; passage of time れきし 歴史 history	厂 a cliff 木 tree; shrub; bush; wood 止 stop The beauty of **a cliff** 厂 with a **tree** 木 does not **stop** 止 with the *passage of time*.
作	**READINGS** **MEANING** **EXAMPLE**	<u>サク</u>・<u>サ</u>・<u>つくる</u>・つくり・~づくり make; production; prepare; build せいさく 製作 manufacture; production	亻 person; man; human 丿 a stroke curved to the left 一 one; a horizontal stroke 丨 line; vertical stroke; rod That **person** 亻 draws **a stroke curved to the left** 丿, then **a horizontal stroke** 一 and a **vertical stroke** 丨 downward to *make* this sign.
送	**READINGS** **MEANING** **EXAMPLE**	<u>ソウ</u>・<u>おくる</u> escort; send ほうそう 放送 broadcasting; broadcast; program	丷 grass; herbs 大 large; big; great; huge 辶 walking; moving They *escort* him to a **grass** 丷 field with **huge** 大 people **walking** 辶 by.
編	**READINGS** **MEANING** **EXAMPLE**	<u>ヘン</u>・<u>あむ</u>・~あみ compilation; knit; plait; braid; twist; editing たんぺん 短編 short (e.g. story, film)	糸 thread; yarn; string 戸 door 冊 counter for books; tome She placed a craft **string** 糸 on a **door** 戸, next to a shelf packed with *compilation* of **tomes** 冊.
輸	**READINGS** **MEANING** **EXAMPLE**	<u>ユ</u>・<u>シュ</u> transport; send; be inferior ゆにゅう 輸入 importation; import; introduction	車 car; automobile; vehicle 人 person; man 一 one; a horizontal stroke 月 moon; month 刂 knife; standing sword This **vehicle** 車 is used to *transport* a **man** 人 for **one** 一 **month** 月, before it will be used to deliver a set of **knife** 刂.

登	**READINGS** **MEANING** **EXAMPLE**	トウ・ト・ドウ・ショ ウ・チョウ・のぼる・ あがる ascend; climb up とうじょう 登場　entry (on stage); appearance (on screen)	癶 dotted tent 豆 legume; bean; pea *Climb up* the **dotted tent** 癶 to view the **bean** 豆 field clearly.
賞	**READINGS** **MEANING** **EXAMPLE**	ショウ・ほめる prize; reward; praise じゅしょう 受賞　winning (a prize)	尚 still; yet; esteem; furthermore 口 mouth; opening; hole; gap 貝 shellfish; seashell; shell **Furthermore** 尚, grab the opportunity to win a *prize* during the market **opening** 口 for **shellfish** 貝 trade.
幅	**READINGS** **MEANING** **EXAMPLE**	フク・はば hanging scroll; width はばひろ 幅広い extensive; wide; broad	巾 width; breadth; towel; cloth 一 one; a horizontal stroke 口 mouth; opening; hole; gap 田 field; rice field The **width** 巾 of **one** 一 *hanging scroll* is as wide as the **opening** 口 of the **field** 田 museum.
愛	**READINGS** **MEANING** **EXAMPLE**	アイ・いとしい・かな しい・めでる・おし む・まな love; affection; favorite れんあい 恋愛 love; romance; affections	爫 claw 冖 crown; cover 心 heart, mind, spirit 夂 strike; hit; folding chair She holds her *favorite* **claw** 爫 **crown** 冖 diamond ring close to her **heart** 心 while sitting on a **folding chair** 夂.
忘	**READINGS** **MEANING** **EXAMPLE**	ボウ・わすれる forget わす 忘れられない unfor- gettable; memorable	亡 deceased, the late, dying, perish 心 heart, mind, spirit Forgetting something is the **perishing** 亡 of one's **mind** 心.

www.ingramcontent.com/pod-product-compliance
Lightning Source LLC
Chambersburg PA
CBHW080853160726
47999CB00009B/3108